THE MOTOR BUS
IN LONDON
1904-8

R. W.

THE OAKWOOD PRESS
1975

911?00000014359

INTRODUCTION

The period from 1904 to 1908 was unique in the history of the London motor bus, for at the beginning of those four years the mechanically-propelled bus was virtually unknown in London, and by the end of them a whole gamut of trial and error had been run, and the scene had set into the almost monopolistic mould that would remain until the 'pirates' came in 1922 to stir things up again.

There had been some early attempts to introduce mechanical buses. In the 1829–1845 period a number of steam buses, notably those of Walter Hancock, had run. In 1891 the Bersey electric bus, manufactured by the Electrical Construction Company of Wolverhampton, had operated briefly from Victoria to Charing Cross. In 1897 Mr. House's Lifu oil-fired steam bus had been tried, and in 1898 a small Daimler bus. Then in 1899 two more Daimlers, fitted with double-deck bodies by Owen, Brazil & Holborow of Bristol (later Straker), were operated by the Motor Traction Co. Ltd. The London Motor Omnibus Syndicate tried out a small Gillette steam bus, and in 1902 put some very small Scott Stirling single-deckers on the Cricklewood to Oxford Circus route. Also in 1902 the London Road Car Co.Ltd., operated a double-deck Thornycroft steam bus for a short time. This was only the tip of a large iceberg of financial promotions seeking to make fortunes out of bringing the motor bus to London, all of which failed. One of these would have brought in an enormous fleet of de Dion steam buses as operated in Paris.

The fact of the matter was that there was no British-built chassis available on which a motor-bus could be mounted. When at the end of the nineteenth century the petrol motor car had "arrived", there was a discussion at an Automobile Club dinner on the subject of heavy motors, between (amongst others) Col. R. E. B. Crompton, at that time the War Office adviser on heavy transport, Mr. S. F. Edge, the pioneer motorist, the Hon. C. S. Rolls and Mr. Sidney Straker; they concluded that no public service vehicle weighing over 30 cwt. unladen and carrying more than fourteen passengers could succeed. Sidney Straker's attempt to run two double-deck Daimlers in 1899 was discouraging enough to confirm this view, and thus motor bus development was largely confined to putting small wagonettes on country routes. In 1901 two comparatively large Daimler petrol lorries were entered in the Liverpool heavy motor trials by Frederick Simms and H. G. Burford, both of Messrs. G. F. Milnes & Co.Ltd. of Birkenhead, and did well enough. Burford got the message; a few years later he was managing director of Milnes-Daimler Ltd. and supplying workable single-deck Daimler motor buses to various provincial operators, including the Great Western Railway. Meanwhile Sidney Straker, who was associated with E. H. Bailey, who had been Chairman of the London Road Car Company, and also with H. J. Lawson, the promoter who had tried to bring de Dion steam buses to London, succeeded in obtaining the British rights of another successful German motor chassis, made by Büssing in Brunswick; together with another engineer called Squire, he joined the Bristol engineering firm of Brazil, Holborow, and early in 1905 was able to deliver his first Büssing bus to the Road Car Company.

While these two companies, Milnes-Daimler and Straker-Squire, were consolidating their plans, Thomas Clarkson, who had developed a good water-tube-boilered steam chassis at Chelmsford, persuaded both the London General and the Road Car Company to try his steam bus, single-decker versions being put in service by each Company within two days of each other in April 1904. London importing agencies had also been busy, and during 1904 some German Durkopps, Swiss Orions, and Belgian Germains came to London; at the beginning of 1904 there were 13 mechanical buses in London, by the end of the year, 31. There was of course some resistance by people with a large capital sunk in horses, and the Metropolitan Police, who exercised a careful (some would say rigid) control on what London buses could or could not do, were worried by these innovations. But even the horse bus owners could see the writing on the wall; motor buses were appearing all over the provinces and the public in London was ready. By the summer of 1905 the number of motor buses had jumped to 73, owned as follows:

London Power	9	Star	3
Tilling	12	H. Turner	2
Road Car	19	New London Suburban	2
London Motor	16	French	1
Birch Bros.	3	Associated	1
London General	4	London & County	1

Suddenly, London was full of budding motor bus companies; to mix metaphors, the flood gates were opened, but only a trickle of chassis was coming through. There was a limit even to the Continental companies' capacity, though they were bending most of their energies on London—Berlin had yet to see its first motor bus. What a frustrating time it must have been for the London agencies: Motor Car Emporium offering Durkopps, Ducommuns, Mors and others; E. & N. Hora squeezing out one Turgan, Moss & Wood frantically praising the merits of the rather puny Orion. They consoled themselves by putting in the press what they would like to believe. Usually it took the form of a photo of a bus stating that a further 100 were on order, but sometimes they said 'as already running in large numbers'. Before long it became clear that only the companies with a manufacturing base, Milnes and Straker, could provide these Continental designs in large enough numbers. And what were the British manufacturers doing? A lot of prototypes were coming out: the Critchley-Norris, the Ailsa Craig, the Durham-Churchill, the Thames—even the Hunslet Engine Company produced a heavy chassis. But they were blown on the wind; and the

Wolseley all-chain-drive model was not a success. By the end of 1905 Leyland in co-operation with Crossley of Manchester had a good bus running, and Dennis of Guildford sold two of their design with final worm drive which looked promising. Some makers, such as Napier, ignored the London market, scared no doubt by the rigid Police specifications. Hallford, who were making the Swiss Saurer, preferred to produce lorries. And a bus was not just a chassis; the failure of Scott Stirling of Twickenham to build two buses a week as promised to the London Power Company may have been partly due to congestion at Brush in Loughborough, who built the bodies for them.

Meanwhile the well-known London horse-bus builder, Christopher Dodson, had tooled up for putting bodies on motor chassis. He had to cope with police regulations and a wide variety of chassis types, but succeeded in producing a useful and reasonably standard body; police regulations at the time required a length over platform not exceeding 23 ft., a wheelbase not exceeding 14 ft. 6 ins., track 5 ft. 6 ins., total width 7 ft. 2 ins., and seating for 18 passengers on top and 16 inside. On a visit to Dodsons in November 1905, the journal 'Motor Traction' found in the body-building bays 3 Pipes, a Turgan, 12 Milnes Daimlers, 25 Strakers, 7 Orions (not all destined for London). In January 1906 Dodsons became a public company.

There was some alarm at the preponderance of foreign makes. The British Empire Motor Traction Alliance was set up to encourage the home product; even at this time it was realised that Britain would need a heavy motor industry in time of War. The Leyland-Crossley, the Dennis and the Wolseley appeared in small numbers. The last-named originally had a two-cylinder engine which caused it to vibrate painfully. A story was published relating how two buses drew up side-by-side in a traffic jam in Piccadilly; a lady on the top deck of a Wolseley was complaining of the vibration, and a Frenchman on the top of the other bus, a Milnes, told her that British buses vibrated, whereas ones from the Continent did not. Whereupon a patriotic Englishman challenged the Frenchman to come with him to Richmond and travel on one of the new London Suburban Leylands, which he would find as smooth as any.

By 1906 there were 26 routes on which motors were running (though of about 500 vehicles involved, nearly one-fifth were on the favourite Cricklewood route). It was now being suggested that fixed stopping places be instituted, and the London Motor Omnibus Co. with the 'Vanguard' fleet adopted large route numbers displayed at front and sides. It had been a source of complaint by the public that while horse-buses tended to be different colours for particular routes, some motor buses were not. At first LGOC had painted its motor buses in at least four different colours for various routes; London & District with their "Arrow" fleet had sought to overcome the problem by painting the arrow itself in differing colours. However, as time went on it became clear that anything which made it difficult to move a bus from one route to another was to be avoided.

Another legacy of the horse-bus was also disposed of; this was time allowed for 'petrolling' which took the place of time previously allowed for changing horses.

Detachable destination boards for front and rear seem to have been invented by Christopher Dodson the body-builder; he stated in October 1907 that by that date some 300 Vanguards and 200 Generals were carrying his patent boards. They carried the two end destinations in large letters at the top and intermediate points in smaller letters below.

There was, of course, a good deal of complaining about rough riding. Regular passengers came to know what streets would give them a severe shaking; one writer to the Press referred to granite setts in the Hammersmith Road as "standing out like precipices". The frequent dense fogs seem to have worried the drivers more than the passengers. One driver who had clearly served most of his life in a different form of transport described a trip in a bad fog thus: "I keep the Trafalgar Square oil flares on my port bow, and then keep the chemist's shop lantern dead ahead until I pick up the Outer Strand light. Trinity House should be spoke to about the Pall Mall Beacon—it's too far west in the channel".

Noise and skidding also came in for frequent mention. The police made frequent but inconclusive noise tests on various makes of bus; the only thing all agreed upon was that the pinion-and-toothed ring final drive of the Milnes-Daimler became very noisy when some years old; some Tilling and LGOC buses were 'silenced' by fitting Dennis worm-drive rear axles. Various anti-skid devices were also tried. In 1906 Road Car fitted some buses with pneumatic tyres on the front, but the drivers would not have them as they made the steering heavy. Some General buses were fitted with wheels having round rubber pads on the surface of the tyre, but these obviously would wear very quickly. The Electrobus Company made great play of the stink from petrol buses and got some support; but it seems the public as a whole were prepared to accept the disadvantages of petrol buses for the improved service they gave.

Apart from the bigger companies, many of the early motor bus undertakings started with too high hopes and too untried vehicles, and by 1906 some had disappeared and others were seeking amalgamation. Too much money had been put into the fleets, which was wasted on high repair costs, excessive competition, some fare-cutting, and various costs associated with the use mainly of imported vehicles, un-standardised and with short lives. By stages the LGOC, which had been to a great extent sitting on the sidelines and watching the others make the mistakes, acquired control of all but a few of the operators. By 1908, with fairly standard fleets of Milnes-Daimlers, de Dions, and Straker-Büssings, many of course acquired from other operators, and with routes organised on the basis of the Vanguard route-numbers, the 'General' was in fairly good shape. Their next development, the setting up at Walthamstow of their own bus factory and the development of the X-type and then the B-type, would bring to London a degree of public transport efficiency that growing traffic badly needed. It is now time to look at the development of the various undertakings in more detail.

LONDON GENERAL OMNIBUS COMPANY LIMITED

Fleet name "General"

The Company was founded in Paris in December 1855, and the horse-buses first appeared on London Streets on 7th January 1856. The LGOC made some experiments with mechanical traction, including a horse-bus converted with a powered front axle, and a Fischer petrol-electric bus; this latter weighed 2½ tons and was too wide to be licensed by Scotland Yard, but it did attempt to run a service early in 1904 from Highbury to Putney. It was stated that it never actually made the whole run, and was sent to the Mortlake depot, where it languished for two years and was then used for some other petrol-electric experiments.

The LGOC became interested in the Clarkson steam buses, and ordered a 14-seat single-decker, which was stabled at their body factory at Caledonian Road and operated on the Hammersmith—Piccadilly route from 10 October 1904; it was withdrawn on 7 June 1905, but some improved double-deckers followed later. At the same time they were looking at the products of the Continental firms, then better advanced than the British, and ordered for trial buses from Orion, Milnes-Daimler, and Büssing. The Company was offered an option on the whole Daimler output, but declined it; this must have been regretted later as the London Motor Omnibus Company took over the contract with beneficial results. The agreement, with the agents the London Motor Car Emporium, had been for 108 buses at 10—15 per month.

The buses did not at first carry "General" on the side; they were mostly red, but some were yellow, blue or olive green, and the name was on a cartouche in the centre of the body with the main destinations each side. The first bus to carry the "General" name was No. EH-R on 23 December 1905.

Being strong in the horse-bus field, the LGOC adopted a method of marking buses by what had been known as 'times' at the front of the body; these comprised three letters, the first denoting the depot, the second the route and the third the order of arrival of the vehicles on the route. The first depots to receive motor buses were A Acton, E Cricklewood, G Swiss Cottage, H Caledonian Road, and 2 (later Z) Mortlake; in 1906 there followed J Islington, L Camden Town, and M Kings Cross. As time went by the alphabet proved too small for some 'times'; there were more than 26 buses on the Hammersmith—Charing Cross route, so after allotting ZMA—ZMZ, a new series was started with ZO—A. In September 1906 the LGOC purchased road license plate numbers LC8600—8699.

Although chassis numbers were also carried, these are not identifiable in photgoraphs, and to deal with the order of buses arriving in service one must relate to the times numbers. By the end of 1906 these had become somewhat confused due to the fact that when a vehicle was moved to another depot it took on a new times 'number', but the following gives a valuable record of the build up of the motor fleet:

JA−A	Clarkson s.d.	10.10.04	EH−P	de Dion	7.12.05
JA−B	Orion (small)	12.04	EH−Q	,,	23.12.05
EL−A	Milnes-Daimler	29. 5.05	EH−R	,,	,,
EH−A	Büssing	,,	GM−A	Milnes-Daimler	1.06
EH−B	Wolseley	1. 7.05	EH−S	de Dion	8. 1.06
EH−C	Orion (ex-JA−B)		LM−A	transferred de	
EH−D	Milnes-Daimler	12. 7.05		Dions	
EH−E	Crossley-Leyland	22. 7.05	LM−B	,,	
EH−A	Orion (improved)	1. 8.05	LM−C	de Dion	15. 1.06
EL−B	Büssing (ex-EH−A)	−	EH−G	Büssing	16. 1.06
EH−F	Crossley-Leyland	1. 8.05	EH−C	de Dion	,,
EH−G	Wolseley	29. 8.05	EH−J	Straker	,,
EH−Z	Milnes-Daimler	,,	GM−B	Milnes-Daimler	24. 1.06
EH−H	Orion	16. 9.05	LM−D	,,	,,
EH−I	Wolseley	22. 9.05	EH−I	Büssing	1. 2.06
EH−K	Brillie	13.10.05	LM−E	Milnes-Daimler	,,
EH−J	Wolseley	19.10.05	EH−B	de Dion	4. 2.06
EH−L	Straker	,,	EH−T	Büssing	,,
EH−M	de Dion	10.05	EH−V	de Dion	9. 2.06
EH−N	,,	8.11.05	EH−W	,,	14. 2.06
EH−O	,,	7.12.05	EH−X	,,	,,

On 18 February 1906 EH−B/G/N/P/R/S/V/W/X were relettered AH−A to AH−I and sent to work the Oxford Circus to West Kensington route.

Eight new de Dions appeared between 24 February and 28 March: EH−B/F/G/N/P/S/V/Z, and three new Büssings, EH−R/X/Y. EH−W was a Wolseley-Siddeley. The old Wolseleys had been withdrawn and this improved version was to be tried out. On 15 March there appeared MG−A, a de Dion for some reason in blue livery, on the Kings Cross to Victoria route; new Milnes for the favourite Cricklewood route were EN−A/B, and to the Childs Hill−Pimlico route went two more de Dions, GK−B/C, and AHJ to O went on to the West Kensington route during Spring 1906. Additions to the Kings Cross route were MG−B/C, both de Dions. Further additions at this time were GK−D, a Milnes, EI−B/C, de Dions, and EH−E and EI−A, Büssings. LO−A/B (de Dions) went on to the Hampstead Heath to Victoria route. AH−P (de Dion) went into service on 23 April. Now the H yard came into use, with HD−A to HD−D, and HD−H/I, new Strakers, and five existing Büssings, EH−I/J/R/T/X, which became HD−J/F/G/E/K.

Transferences and new vehicles continued hard and fast; suffice to say that at the end of August Mortlake came into service with de Dions 2M−A to 2M−G, only the last being new; the figure 2 later gave place to the letter Z. De Dions, Strakers and Büssings continued to arrive in almost equal numbers, and five new Clarkson steamers, S, S—A to S—D arrived at Bow to work Canning Town to Oxford Circus, in November.

Despite this belated arrival of the Clarksons, it was clear that the LGOC had, after their two years of trial and error, opted for the Büssing design. Although originally the German Büssings and the British Strakers (virtually the same machine) had been regarded as inseparable, in August 1906 the LGOC decided to separate them, and made Acton a Büssing depot and Caledonian Road a Straker one. There seems to be no way of telling externally the difference between what the LGOC regarded as a Büssing or a Straker-Squire, but references in the press suggest that the title "Büssing" was applied to some of the early 24 H.P. LGOC models which had probably been imported direct from Brunswick—though perhaps on paper via Strakers—and also to the 40 H.P. models, referred to as "the big new Büssings" which were going into service from June 1905 onwards. Probably there were minor differences in spares which made it sensible for the LGOC to separate the German-built and the Bristol-built versions. From about 1908 both types were fitted with new radiators with large header-tanks which made it even more difficult at a glance to tell the original provenance of the bus; most were probably the larger of the two standard Straker chassis, the 34 H.P.; the 40 H.P. could be recognised by having a rounded instead of square top to the bonnet.

From October 1906 buses began to appear with their chassis number reclassified and united with the body number; henceforth it was painted in red on black on the offside frame member, and also in white on the bonnet. The makes in use were classified as follows: from 1, Büssing, 01 Milnes-Daimler, 101 Straker and 201 de Dion, 301 Wolseleys, 401 Clarksons. Actually, Nos. 01 to 019 were reserved for some oldsters which were still around, the one and only Brillié, the Orions, and the Crossley-Leylands now working as service vehicles. When early in 1907 a Ryknield was put on trial, this was allotted 019. Next year, when amalgamations began, this simplistic numbering system was not up to the job, and various types were allotted letter prefixes (P for Büssings for example); the 'times' boards were however continued in use for depot purposes.

Some experimenting continued. A petrol-electric bus with Wolseley-Siddeley engine and electrical equipment by BT-H of Rugby (LN 4501) was put on the Barnes—Canning Town route, in September 1907. In October 1908 a steam bus was purchased from the firm of Bellis & Morcom, and this was run on route 16 alongside a de Dion fitted with a Clarkson steam engine (No. 412) to enable comparison to be made between the two systems. Three Beaufort buses appeared briefly in LGOC livery; two were ZR—Z and ZR—Y on the Barnes to Oxford Circus route; it seems however that Scotland Yard did not pass them.

The decision to amalgamate with Vanguard was taken in effect at the board meetings of the Companies in March 1908, though their vehicles continued to operate in their own livery. However, the Vanguard route numbering system was adopted by the LGOC, and the Vanguard works at Walthamstow was re-equipped by the LGOC for the manufacture of complete buses (and later made a separate concern as the Associated Equipment Company). Here in 1909 the Chief Engineer Frank Searle (an ex-Arrow and Vanguard man) was to produce the X-type bus, loosely based on the Leyland live-axle design, followed in 1910 by the famous B-type. However, for the time being the LGOC was occupied in digesting the varied fleets of the former independent companies, which were allotted initial letters, for instance A, D, and E for ex-Vanguard Milnes, F and G for ex-Union Jack Strakers, K ex-MOC Armstrong-Whitworths, L, M and N de Dions (some ex-Vanguards), R various Maudsleys, T ex-Great Eastern Arrol-Johnsons, Y ex-Great Eastern late Strakers.

The ex-Independents continued to serve for many years, often in rather butchered form; this period during which a great number of General buses ran with odd wheels, odd radiators and an overall scruffy appearance is usually glossed over in 'official' histories, but until the arrival of sufficient numbers of the B-type the motley collection had to keep pace with rising demand as the horse-buses were phased out. Meanwhile, on the financial front the LGOC were becoming involved in complex deals and also confrontation with the tramway interests, from which it emerged unscathed, to sell itself profitably to the Underground Group in 1912.

THE LONDON ROAD CAR COMPANY LIMITED

Fleet name "Union Jack"

The Company was formed in 1879, and for the first year was known as "The London & District Omnibus Co.". It adopted an emblem of crossed Union Jacks, to emphasise its opposition to the French-owned London General Omnibus Company, and after 1905 its motor buses carried the fleet name "Union Jack" on their sides. This was one of the first bus companies to recognise the need for mechanical propulsion, even though it was the owner of a large fleet of horse buses, and on 17th March 1902 it began running a Thornycroft double-deck steam-bus on its Hammersmith—Oxford Circus route. This was not successful, and was sold; the Company then ordered three petrol-electric buses from America, but they were never delivered. Also in 1902 they built a petrol-driven tractor at their own Fulham Works, but were not satisfied, and ordered three of the new German Milnes-Daimler buses. Again, these were not delivered, and the Company turned to Thomas Clarkson, whose 'Chelmsford' steam buses were being actively promoted. They ordered two single-deck buses at the same time as the LGOC ordered one, but they got their buses on the road two days before their rivals, on 8th October 1904. This was a two-cylinder paraffin-fired type, and the route was the Hammersmith to Oxford Circus one (later extended to Charing Cross). These cars carried numbers S1 and S2. On 5th September 1905 the Company put on the road their first double-deck 32 h.p. Clarkson; at the same time they were trying out their first Durkopp petrol bus, an early version of this marque with a short body.

The Company placed further orders for both Clarksons and Durkopps, as well as for the Belgian Germain. This last seems to have been a mistake, for though the Germains seemed quick on delivery, they were a constant source of trouble. The make was not well-tried, and most of them had to be returned to Belgium for modifications. Even the improved version proved to be incapable of breasting Notting Hill at an acceptable speed, and they were transferred to the less hilly route between Putney and Oxford Circus. From March 1905 orders were also placed for Straker-Squire buses, which were successful and enabled the Hammersmith route to be continued through the City to Burdett Road, Mile End. At the Company's half-yearly meeting in August 1905, it reported that there were 28 motor-buses on the road, and that they had carried about one million of the 37 million passengers catered for in the year. The buses carried a Union Jack on a short pole mounted over the driver's cab, and became very popular on the streets. Still in search for the best vehicle, the Company ordered some of the newly-introduced Maudsleys, though none seem to have been on the road before well into 1906.

From photographs, it would appear that at first numbers were allotted by make: the first Clarkson carried S1, and later apparently the two Clarkson single-deckers were numbered MC1/2; some Strakers carried Q numbers. However, the official fleet list for the first 100 or so buses seems to have been as follows:

1	Clarkson (s.d.)	1904
2	Durkopp	1904
3	Germain	11/1904
4	Durkopp	12/1904
5	,,	2/1905
6	Büssing	9/3/1905

This ended the experimental phase and up to the end of 1905 the following went into service:

7–13	Durkopp		40	Durkopp
14–15	Germain		41	Straker
16–17	Durkopp		42	Durkopp
18	Germain		43	Straker
19	Durkopp		44	Durkopp
20–25	Germain		45–48	Straker
26–28	Durkopp		49	Durkopp
29	Germain		50	Straker
30–31	Durkopp		51	Durkopp
35–37	Straker		52–53	Straker
38	Durkopp		54	Durkopp
39	Straker		55–56	Straker

57	Durkopp	102	Clarkson
58–65	Straker	103	Straker
(end of 1905)		104	Clarkson
		105	Straker
66–67	Clarkson	106	Maudslay
68	Straker	107	Straker
69	Clarkson	108	Maudslay
70–73	Straker	109	Straker
74	Clarkson	110	Maudslay
75–83	Straker	111	Straker
84	Durkopp	112	Clarkson
85	Clarkson	113	Straker
86–88	?	114	Clarkson
89	Clarkson	115	Maudslay
90–96	Straker	116	Clarkson
97	Clarkson	117–118	Straker
98	Maudslay	119	Maudslay
99	Straker	120–126	Straker
100	Clarkson		
101	Straker		

This brings the list up to the autumn of 1906; further numbers are not available but it is believed the new deliveries were mainly Strakers, though Maudslays operated on the Clapham Junction–Highbury Barn Service. The livery of the buses seems to have varied according to route: those on the Clapham Junction–Highbury route were yellow.

In February 1908 Union Jack decided that they could get no further use from their Germains, which according to the records had not been on the road for over a year, and advertised them for sale. At the same time they introduced a new type of Durkopp with Straker engine (No. A8237). By the summer the fleet was under LGOC control, though running still in Union Jack livery. The buses were given LGOC fleet numbers; the numbers were painted in white on the bonnet sides. The official date of amalgamation was 1 July 1908.

LONDON MOTOR OMNIBUS COMPANY LIMITED

Fleet name "Vanguard"

This Company was the first to take motor buses in London really seriously, and at first appeared the most successful. Starting with a capital of £60,000, the first bus was put on the road in April 1905. The route was Brondesbury to Waterloo, and by July there were 17 Milnes Daimlers and one 2– cylinder Wolseley in service. In August the London to Brighton route was inaugurated by No. 29, using Milnes Daimlers, later Scheiblers, and also a single-deck Milnes.

Another route was started, from the Old Kent Road to Cricklewood, and also Finchley Road to Ebury Bridge. The Company was full of ideas; one was to run buses from Dieppe to Monte Carlo, but this failed to get

going. Private hire work was undertaken and Vanguard buses carried boys
of the Rugby School Mission to summer camp at New Romney in 1905.
In November 1905 trials were carried out with the Simms-Welbeck bus,
built by the Simms Manufacturing Co. of Kilburn. In general Vanguard
remained faithful to Milnes Daimlers, having taken over an option on
output which had been rejected by the LGOC. The buses did not originally
carry fleet numbers, as a block of registrations from A9101 to A9200 had
been obtained. By 1907 according to Milnes Daimler advertising Vanguard
had no less than 282 of their buses, but there were also a few De Dions
and Thornycrofts.

New routes were opened up: Victoria to St. Johns Wood, extended
to Ebury Bridge and to Finchley Road; Tufnell Park to Barnes Common;
Victoria to Hampstead Heath; Gospel Oak to Putney Town. This was
the only Company to carry route numbers, black on white discs on the
front and sides. The depots were at Camberwell Green (Route 1),
Albany Street (Routes 2, 4, 6, 7) and Kings Cross (Routes 3 and 8);
later a depot was opened at Shepherds Bush to cater for route 4. Route
numbers proliferated, and the famous and still present route 16 first
appeared on a Vanguard.

Vanguard had a flare for publicity, as in January 1906 when they
allowed the actress Kate Cutler to use No. A9101 as a mobile dressing
room to do two shows in different theatres. In 1906 also a number of
Vanguards were sent to Epsom to act as grandstands for the Derby.
In the summer of 1906 Vanguard began operating the first of a new type
of Milnes-Daimler, with four-speed instead of three-speed gearbox; this
bus (LC5061) was however on provisional license for several months as
the police for some reason had difficulty in passing it.

In August 1906 the Company obtained a new double-chain-drive
Thornycroft, but it is believed this was not passed by the police. De Dions
appeared in 1907; in December of that year amalgamation was announced
with London & District, the London Motor Bus Co., and London &
Provincial. All these companies appear to have been under the control of
one person, Mr. A.T. Salisbury Jones, and it was felt at the time that it
would have been better if they had not been set up as separate companies.
The Company was reconstituted as The Vanguard Motor Bus Company,
and the livery was changed in that the side panels carried the words
"Vanguard Service" instead of the previous old-fashioned lettering inside
a banner outline.

In June 1907 some new Armstrong-Whitworth buses appeared in the
Vanguard fleet and at least one Arrol-Johnston; meanwhile the three
Scheiblers had apparently been converted to 1200-gallon tankers to carry
fuel from Silvertown to the Company's depots. The depot at Walthamstow,
later to become the LGOC factory, was very well-appointed, and published
figures suggest that Vanguard succeeded in keeping a high proportion of
their buses in service at all times. Nevertheless the Company, which now

had 389 buses, was not making a profit, and had some very unhappy shareholders. In March 1908 it was agreed that the only way out was to make a working agreement with the LGOC and to write down some of the excessive capital. The fusion was officially effective from 1 July, though the buses continued for some time in their own livery. By the autumn, Vanguard shares (still quoted separately) were down to 9d. for the £1 shares, a sad ending for a Company which seemed to have done more to popularise the motor bus than any other London concern.

THOMAS TILLING LTD.

Fleet name "Tilling"

Thomas Tilling began running horse-buses between Peckham and Oxford Circus in 1847; after he died in 1893 the concern became a public company.

Tillings were well disposed towards motors, in spite of their large horse-bus and livery stable business, and were fortunate in having the well-known P. Frost Smith as Engineer. Purchase of horses ceased in 1905.

The early motor fleet was as follows:

1	Milnes-Daimler	30/9/1904
2	,,	10/1904
3	,,	,,
4	,,	12/1904
5	,,	,,
6–9	,,	3/1905
–	Büssing	5/1905
10	Milnes-Daimler	,,
11–13	Milnes-Daimler mail-vans	
14	Milnes-Daimler	7/1905
15	old M-D (lorry)	
16	Milnes-Daimler	7/1905
17–19	Straker 20 h.p.	9/1905
20	,, 28 h.p.	,,
21	cabs	
22	Milnes-Daimler	1/1906
23–24	cabs	
25	Milnes-Daimler	3/1906

From here a number of Dennis buses were mixed in with new Strakers and Panhard cabs and the numbering became somewhat confusing. The number was painted on each side of the bonnet and on the rear frame members. Livery varied according to route, but owing to difficulties in interchanging vehicles it was decided at the end of 1905 to paint all buses olive green and to have a coloured board on the main side panels varying by route; the board was green for Peckham—Oxford Circus, red for Peckham—Lewisham. This latter route was extended to Lee after a long tussle with the LCC Tramways whose tramway-building activities made some streets impassable. Six new Dennis buses with Tyler engines were put into service in September 1906.

Milnes-Daimler No.4 was converted with a Dennis worm drive rear axle to reduce noise, and this may have been done to others.

At first Tillings worked in the Atlas and Waterloo 'Association' on a route from Elephant to Finchley Road (later Marylebone station) but quitted it in December 1906. The Tilling fleet did not build up as fast as some others, and by 1908 comprised only 36 buses.

In 1907 Frost Smith became interested in a petrol-electric system devised by W. A. Stevens, a Maidstone engineer, and one bus on this system was built by the old-established firm of J. & E. Hall at Dartford, at that time building lorries under the Swiss Saurer patents. This was put into service by Tillings in January 1908, but it was three years before the Maidstone-built production vehicle, the TTA1, came on the streets. Thereafter all Tilling buses were petrol-electric until 1928. Tillings entered into agreements with the LGOC in 1909 and from May 1912 were limited to 150 buses within the General-controlled 'pool', retaining their own livery.

LONDON POWER OMNIBUS COMPANY LIMITED

Fleet name "Pioneer"

The Company began in 1902 as the London Motor Omnibus Syndicate, running small single-deck Scott-Stirling buses between Cricklewood and Oxford Circus. These were not very successful, but in 1905 Mr. John Stirling, who had allegedly been responsible for running the first motor bus (at Lanark in 1896) decided to extend operations, under the fleet name "Pioneer". A fleet of double-deck Scott-Stirling buses was obtained, together with at least one single-decker rather larger than the original ones. The Scott-Stirling was an odd-looking vehicle, with the radiator mounted high in front of the driver (later versions had double radiators), and in later models iron wheel felloes. The first double-deckers carried 16 inside, 18 outside, and 2 on a box seat in front. In February 1906 a very large depot was opened at Cricklewood. By 1907 there were 63 buses in service, but the Company was plagued by disputes with the manufacturers, Scott-Stirling of Twickenham, mostly about late deliveries. (In 1906 Scott-Stirling had announced an amalgamation with Argyll of Glasgow, yet in May 1907 a new company, Scott-Stirling Motor Co., was set up.) It seems probable that the close tie-up between London Power and the makers was the root of their troubles. In any case, they went off the road in the summer of 1907.

LONDON & DISTRICT MOTOR BUS COMPANY LIMITED

Fleet name "Arrow"

The Company began operating in October 1905, with Straker-Squire buses. Each bus carried a large arrow on a pole above the cab, the colour of this denoting the route (Putney to Charing Cross had a white arrow). The depot was at Farm Lane, Walham. There was at this time some accrimonious correspondence in the Press regarding whether the Arrow buses ought to be called Straker-Squires or Büssings. Sydney Straker had acquired the license to build the Büssing type in Bristol, and for some time it was not clear whether any particular vehicle was a German import or a home-built job. Later Arrow fitted some of these buses with "Albany" radiators, thus somewhat altering their appearance (LC 2238 was so treated in May 1907). Arrow also purchased several Milnes-Daimlers from an operator in the Isle of Wight. In July 1906 three Lacoste & Battman buses were purchased, but these were transferred to the subsidiary Company London & Provincial Motor Bus Company Limited, and replaced by Arrol-Johnsons, also a Beaufort was tried out. By the end of 1906 Arrow had 159 buses, but shortly afterwards was absorbed by Vanguard.

THE MOTOR OMNIBUS COMPANY LIMITED

Fleet name "Pilot"

The Company, floated by A.T. Salisbury-Jones in November, 1905, started in July 1906 with 12 buses, on the Upper Clapton to Peckham route, using 32 h.p. Mors buses with bodies by the United Electric Car Co. Later some Milnes Daimler and De Dion Buses were added, and another route opened between Dalston Junction and Elephant. The livery was bright green with a red band along the main panel. A depot for 180 buses was started in 1907, but the Company joined up with Vanguard and ran for a time in their own livery but carrying Vanguard route numbers, mainly on Route 1 (Brondesbury-Charing Cross). In December 1906 they had obtained some Stoewer bus chassis, but these probably did not all go into service; there is a photo of a Stoewer (LC8512) in service.

THE STAR OMNIBUS COMPANY LIMITED

Fleet name "Star"

The Company was founded in 1899; a beginning with motor buses seems to have been made in the summer of 1905; at this time it was announced that the Company had purchased two French Mors buses, but

The Road Car Company's first Straker Bussing, No.6, which went into service in March 1905

One of the first LGOC Strakers, EH-A (A9008), which went into service on 29 May 1905

A Road Car Germain in original form

"Kingsway" Leyland-Crossley No.P2251 in December 1905 in the newly-opened Kingsway street

An early LGOC de Dion; the number has been blanked out, but it is probably EH-M

*Road Car Clarkson
No.LC2320*

*"Union Jack"
Durkopp No.LC2345*

*"Tilling" No.6, a
Milnes-Daimler, which
went into service in
March 1905*

"Rapide" Ducommun No. 7 (LC3412) in January 1906

Three "Victoria" Orions: No. V36 (in service 6 Sept. 1905), V37 (29 Nov.) V35 (23 Aug.)

An "Arrow" Straker, No.LC2206, on the Putney-Waterloo route

One of Sharland's Clarkson steam buses

A Scott-Stirling double-page advertisement in Motor Traction, 5 April 1906. On the right, 'Pioneer' double-decker No.14; bottom left, an older wooden-wheeled s.d. 'Pioneer' No.11;

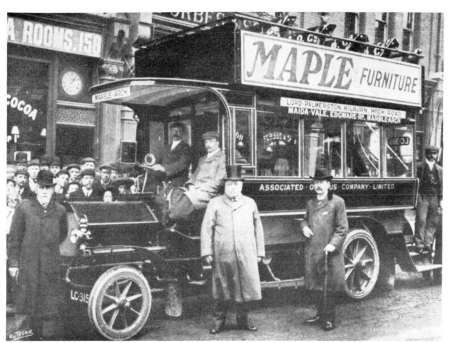

"Associated" Milnes-Daimler No.LC315 in June 1905; all three men in front were Directors of the Company

A four-cylinder Wolseley Siddeley of the LGOC, EH-W, which went on to service in March 1906

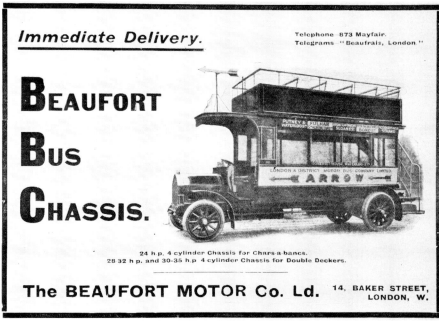
Beaufort No.LC2225 in "Arrow" livery in 1906

"Vanguard's" early single-chain-drive Thornycroft No.A9117

"Star" Brillie No.6

*P. Hearn's Durkopp
(LC4392) outside
the National Gallery*

*MOC ("Pilot") Mors
No.LC7312 (UEC
body) in 1906*

A Vanguard Scheibler in 1906 (LC5017)

"Vanguard" Milnes-Daimler No.LN315

Probably the first Dennis worm-drive bus in London; No.B of London & Suburban (Kingsway) in May 1905

"Standard" Lacoste & Battman LC6677 on the Finsbury Park to Hammersmith service in September 1906

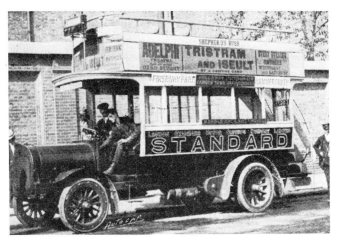

"Union Jack" Maudslay No.LC4136 in June 1906

"Vanguard" drivers being shown the workings of the Milnes-Daimler engine in July 1905, probably in the Walthamstow works

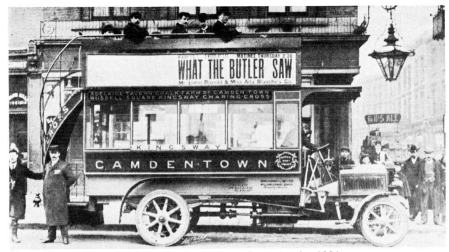

Birch Brothers Leyland-Crossley in October 1906

Electrobus No.LN716 in Fleet Street about 1907, being passed by Vanguard Milnes-Daimler No.A9175

Four Leylands of the "Central" fleet: P2994 and LN189-191

"General" Straker LC3760 bearing the 1906 number 106, and with rebuilt radiator and solid front wheels

The petrol-electric Hallford-Stevens in "Tilling" livery: forerunner of the large Tilling-Stevens p/e fleet

"Union Jack" Straker No.LN261 carrying the Vanguard route number 3 (extended to Whyteleafe) and also carrying LGOC bonnet number G12

The LGOC Belliss & Morcom steam bus LN4509, 1908, here seen on the Hammersmith-Canning Town route

LGOC de Dion-Clarkson No.412 on trial on route 16 in 1908

An evocative view of a "General" Milnes-Daimler LC900 braving the slush at Charing Cross about 1907

An "Electrobus" with covered top 1908; it was definitely seen in service, but it is not certain that this passed Scotland Yard scrutiny (from "Pennyfare" magazine, June 1935)

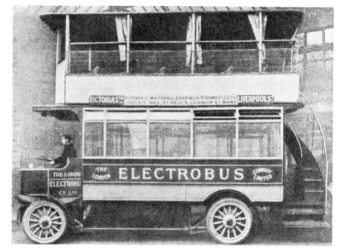

A "Great Eastern" Arrol-Johnston on the Seven Kings-Elephant route in April 1907

this was denied by the British Agent for Mors. There were four Milnes Daimlers running on the Peckham to Oxford Circus route, and at least one Lacoste & Battmann was added in July 1906. Twenty-two Brilliés were ordered, but it is doubtful if all were delivered. The route was altered to run from Camberwell to the Eyre Arms. The fleet number was painted on the front of the cab sheeting; the first Brillié was No. 6. As early as March 1906 the Company was appealing for someone to amalgamate with them; at the end of that year it had 23 buses. Motor buses were withdrawn in Sept. 1907, but 150 horse-buses continued for a further year.

BIRCH BROTHERS LIMITED

This old horse-bus concern, part of the Atlas & Waterloo Association, started running two Milnes-Daimlers on 11th October, 1904, on the North Finchley to Oxford Circus route; they also worked Kings Cross to Victoria and and Camden Town to Charing Cross. A de Dion (No. LC4813) followed early in 1906, and the buses ran in their own livery rather than Atlas & Waterloo; another Milnes Daimler (LC 7590) came in July 1906; some new 40 H.P. Leylands were purchased, also in 1906, and by May 1907 there were 16 buses in the fleet. As befits a horse-bus operator, there was no fleet name on the sides, only the destinations. All buses were withdrawn on 24th October, 1907, and the Company did not return to the London streets until 1922.

LONDON ELECTROBUS COMPANY LIMITED

Fleet name "Electrobus"

The first bus, LC 5768, was run on 20 April 1906, the chassis was by the Improved Electric Traction Co., and had a 14 h.p. BTH motor; accumulators supplied current at 90 volts, and 20 miles could be run between charging. It seems that some 1902 patents had been acquired from the London Motor Car Emporium, with some shadowy foreign characters in the background, for £20,000. The Company was registered with a capital of £305,000, but the trade press of the time cast doubts on the whole undertaking; they believed that the patents infringed some taken out much earlier by Thornycroft, and such was the weight of disapproval that Electrobus offered to return shareholders their money. Many took this offer, and some took the Company to the High Court claiming misrepresentation in the prospectus. By April 1908 the press was still rumbling that after spending £50,000 the Company only had twelve buses; the price paid for the chassis £700 was thought to be excessive. However, by the end of the year there were 19 buses, at least one with covered top deck. As was usual in these cases, though the Electrobus had made its debut with much publicity, its demise in 1910 did not attract much attention. It is believed that a few went to work in Brighton.

GREAT EASTERN LONDON MOTOR OMNIBUS COMPANY LIMITED

Fleet name "Great Eastern"

The origin of this undertaking was The Great Eastern London Suburban Tramways & Omnibus Co., really an offshoot of the Leyton Tramways, and service began in late 1905 with 34 H.P. Strakers on the Upton Park to Oxford Circus route. A company was formed in June 1906 called the Great Eastern London Motor Omnibus Company, with a capital of £405,000. Some Dennis buses were purchased early in 1906, more Strakers (with Brush bodies) and in 1908 several Arrol-Johnsons; the fleet totalled 74 by the autumn of that year. New routes were opened up, including Seven Kings to Elephant in 1908, and the Company was moderately successful. Nevertheless it fell into the LGOC net, being officially absorbed on 1st January 1911. The Arrol-Johnson were given numbers prefixed T by the LGOC, and some late Strakers the letter Y. It is not clear whether any Dennises were taken over: livery was red with gold lettering.

THE ATLAS & WATERLOO ASSOCIATION

One bus, a Milnes-Daimler begain running for this well established horse bus syndicate in September 1904, on the Baker Street to Waterloo route; soon there were also three Milnes Daimlers on the North Finchley to Oxford Circus route. The syndicate included one Birch Brothers bus and eleven Clarkson buses of Burtwell and Sharland. It ceased operating some time in 1907, though three Burtwell buses continued on the route independently for some time.

THE NEW LONDON & SUBURBAN MOTOR OMNIBUS COMPANY LIMITED

Fleet name "Kingsway"

This concern started in October 1905 on a route between Richmond and Kingston. The fleet 'numbers' comprised letters on the side behind the roof canopy, and A was an early Leyland-Crossley with unusual small radiator; B was one of the first (if not the first) worm-drive Dennis in London. Some further Leyland-Crossleys were purchased with a new type of radiator having serrated top to the header-tank. In 1906 four of the new 40 H.P. Leylands were added. When the new Kingsway from Theobalds Road to Aldwych was opened in the autumn of 1905 the fleet ran down it on a new route from Haverstock Hill to Law Courts, and adopted the fleet name 'Kingsway'. In spite of owning buses which passengers regarded as superior in comfort to most others, the company went off the road in 1907.

THE VICTORIA MOTOR OMNIBUS COMPANY LIMITED

Fleet name "The Old Vics"

This undertaking was started by the sons of two horse-bus operators, Messrs. Glover and Cane, in August 1905 on the Kilburn to Law Courts route, using the Swiss Orions, small buses which carried only 25 passengers. They were stated to be built short in length to make them handier in traffic (the driver sat over the engine as in the Germain). From 6th September, 1905 they were operating between Cricklewood and Victoria. Most buses only carried the company name, but a photograph of No. V40 has the fleet name "The Old Vics" on the side. Numbering presumably started at V32 as returns showed only 9 buses; No. V40 (LC2370) was exhibited at the Commercial Motor Show in March 1906 by Moss & Wood. By spring of 1908 the company had disappeared from the streets.

ASSOCIATED OMNIBUS COMPANY LIMITED

Fleet name "Associated"

This was one of the earlier operators, starting about the summer of 1905, on the Kilburn—Law Courts and Charing Cross—Finchley routes. Milnes-Daimlers were used, and there was one Cremorne fitted with an ex-horse-bus body. A Rolls-Metallurgique was also operated, but possibly not for long. In December £50,000 of debentures were issued to cover new vehicles and a new garage was opened at Whitcher Place, Camden Town, to house 50 buses. At least one Milnes-Daimler (LC 315) was shedded at the LGOC Cricklewood depot. There were 27 buses by the end of 1906.

The new buses were from de Dion, Straker and more Milnes-Daimlers. But the Company did not prosper and paid no dividend in 1907; its history between this time and its official absorption into the LGOC pool on 2nd October 1912 is not clear; it was purchased by the LGOC on 18th January 1918.

LONDON CENTRAL OMNIBUS COMPANY LIMITED

Fleet name "Central"

This concern was floated in April 1906, apparently with Leyland backing, and its Leyland fleet started on the Chalk Farm to Waterloo route in November, working in conjunction with London & Suburban. The buses were painted dark blue, with 'Central' on a red cartouche. By 1912 agreement had been reached with the LGOC and the Company was re-registered as "New Central"; operation was taken over by the LGOC on 1 January 1913, who completed purchase on 1 July 1914.

RAPID ROAD TRANSIT COMPANY LIMITED

Fleet name "Rapide"

The Company began running twelve Ducommuns obtained from the Motor Car Emporium, on 1st February, 1906, on the Hammersmith to Piccadilly route. They were handsomely painted in a light colour, and had the fleet number painted in black on the inside of the staircase. They seem to have ceased to run in May and were sold to "Ensign".

THE LONDON & WESTMINSTER
MOTOR OMNIBUS COMPANY LIMITED

Fleet name "Ensign"

This company took over the Ducommuns of Rapide in July 1906, and repainted them, though they got little service from these clumsy giants. It was stated that they intended to operate them in summer at Hastings and Margate. By the autumn the service was at a standstill, either because the Ducommuns were out of service, or had gone to Hastings. (The same company owned the 'Memorial' fleet in Hastings and intended at one time to run these in London also.) Shortly afterwards service was re-opened using Lacoste & Battmann buses (five).

PROVINCIAL MOTOR OMNIBUS COMPANY LIMITED
LONDON & PROVINCIAL MOTOR OMNIBUS COMPANY LIMITED

These companies were both associated with the Arrow concern; in April 1906 they were merged to form the London & Provincial Motor Omnibus Co. Ltd. This latter company took over three Lacoste & Battman buses in 1906 from London & District, but it is believed they ran in "Arrow" livery.

PATRICK HEARN

A well-known firm in private hire, P. Hearn operated five Milnes Daimlers in 1906 from the Dun Cow, down the Old Kent Road, to Finchley Station. There were 9 buses by November 1906. A few buses also operated by Tom Hearn.

THE LONDON STANDARD OMNIBUS COMPANY LIMITED

Fleet name "Standard"

This company began operating in September 1906 on the Hammersmith to Finsbury Park and Stamford Hill to Clapham Common routes, using Lacoste & Battmann buses, painted bright red with "Standard" in large white outline letters. The buses had single seats only on the near side of the top deck; this was supposed to counteract 'lean' due to the camber of the road. There were 7 buses in 1907, but some time in 1908 the fleet vanished. It was under the same management as "Ensign".

BALLS BROTHERS

This small outfit began on 22nd May, 1906 with a Turgan; this unusual bus was in London the previous November but probably on trial. The route was Streatham Common to Oxford Circus; two Lacoste & Battmann buses were added, but by 1908 return show only one Balls Bros. vehicle working.

CAMDEN TOWN OMNIBUS ASSOCIATION

It is recorded that this association ran workmens buses at low fares, starting out at 5.30 a.m.; it is not known what vehicles were used, though there is a record of some de Dions being ordered in 1905.

THE CITY & SUBURBAN MOTOR OMNIBUS COMPANY

Known to have run de Dions in 1905 on the Oxford Circus to Brixton Route.

J.H. GARLE

All that is known is that this operator ran at least one Germain on the Brondesbury to Marble Arch route, from August 1905.

HENRY TURNER

Operated two Milnes Daimlers between Peckham and Oxford Circus.

THE LONDON & COUNTY MOTOR BUS COMPANY

This firm operated on the Oxford Circus to Brixton route but is thought to have ceased working before the end of 1905. At times the buses went as far out as Croydon. They were Strakers.

JOHN SHARLAND & SONS

This operator only ran Clarkson steamers, the first going into service in March 1906 on the Kilburn route; there were 5 by February 1907.

BURTWELL BROTHERS

Also a Clarkson fleet; the first ran in January 1906, and 5 more arrived by April 1907. They worked in with Atlas & Waterloo as stated above. Messrs. C.S. Burtwell had a depot for horse buses in the New Kent Road, but it is not known whether the steamers used this at all; as with other Clarksons, they were serviced by the makers. Three buses continued after the break-up of Atlas & Waterloo.

AMALGAMATED MOTOR BUS COMPANY LIMITED

This undertaking is shown as having 3 buses in 1907 and 5 in 1908; it was formed in 1906 under British Automobile Development auspices and ran a few Brush buses from February 1907. BAD later became BET and formed the Tramways (MET) Omnibus Co. Ltd. which falls outside the period under review.

FREDERICK NEWMAN

Began on 22nd May 1906 with a de Dion between Peckham and Oxford Circus; he had three buses throughout 1906–8.

ROYAL BLUE

Said to have worked from Kings Cross to Victoria, and from Sept. 1906 to Finsbury Park.

NATIONAL

This undertaking is really outside the period being considered, though the vehicles concerned, Clarkson steamers, were being operated privately on hire in 1908. It is said the fleet name was adopted as Clarkson had supplied these buses on hire to the War Office for troop movement trials in 1908/9. In 1909 the National Steam Car Co. Ltd. was formed, and steam buses under the National fleet name were on the streets until 1919, from December 1913 as part of the LGOC pool.

CHARLES FRENCH

Shown as having 2 buses at the end of 1906. Apparently not connected with W.F. French who ran wagonettes in Streatham in 1901 and was later connected with the 'Southdown' concern.

MELLISH & BOFFIN

Shown as having 2 buses at the end of 1906.

THE GEARLESS MOTOR OMNIBUS COMPANY LIMITED

This company was promoted in 1906 by Daimler, to operate the Knight — Pieper — Lanchester petrol-electric bus, one of which was built. Owing to Police objections, and doubts about the patents, the matter lapsed. However, as a result of deals between Daimler, Tilling and BET, from 1913 some normal Daimlers did carry the Gearless fleet-name as part of the LGOC pool. The Company was officially operated by LGOC from 5th April, 1913 and purchased 1st January, 1922.

THE METROPOLITAN STEAM OMNIBUS COMPANY LIMITED

This concern operated Darracq-Serpollet steam buses, with flash boilers developed by the famous Leon Serpollet. The Company did not commence operating until October 1907 on a route from Hammersmith to Charing Cross, initially with 3 buses; they were well-appointed and silent running. There were twenty buses by May 1908, but operations consistently showed a loss. In 1909 26 single-deck buses were built, and early in 1910 some lighter double-deckers. In 1911 a new garage was built in Lots Road, Chelsea, and around 60 buses were in service when in 1912 it was decided to cease operating. The goodwill was taken over by the LGOC on 16th October, 1912, but the buses were probably sold; three turned up in the Isle of Wight. The Company had been fully backed by the Manufacturers, and they sold very few buses elsewhere, probably due to the nervousness many people felt regarding the high pressures used in flash boilers.

RAILWAY-OWNED BUSES

In 1905/6 various railway companies acquired powers to run buses. In the summer of 1905 a Thornycroft was running from St. Pancras to Victoria under Midland Railway and LBSC ownership. The LNWR had a number of Milnes Daimlers, mostly working in the Watford area. Some de Dions worked between Victoria and Piccadilly with the fleet name LNWR-Midland-Gt Northern on their sides.

CONCLUSION

The end of the four years under review here saw the remaining motor bus operators in considerable disarray. Most of the large amount of capital put into the buses by the public and the operators themselves had been lost. There were many reasons; principally the rushing on to the streets of too many types of untried vehicles. In addition, maintenance had been badly organised, and ruinous competition allowed on some routes. The only answer was to unify control and to develop a standard vehicle. The LGOC was in the strongest position financially, and the responsibility fell to this Company. It had been as ruthless as the rest in crowding competitors off the streets, so it was a practical rather than a moral victory. From 1908 the LGOC controlled virtually the whole of London's bus traffic, and by 1910 it had in the new B type a live-axle bus of undoubted reliability. The old Continental buses swept up by amalgamation soldiered on, often heavily rebuilt, until the War, but one cannot escape the conclusion that if the foreign makers had been less eager to pour their products into London during the period under review, the motor bus would have developed more slowly but on sounder lines. Nevertheless the 1904—1908 period takes its place as one of the most colourful in the history of London's buses; a time when a driver could sign a letter to the papers "Sharland No. 5", when a citizen could write of the disgraceful attempts by the 'General' to compete down Southampton Row with his beloved 'Centrals' — a time which would be briefly relived from 1922 when the 'pirates' attempted to break the 'General' monopoly, with some success until the coming of London Transport showed that in the end 'God is always with the Big Battalions'.

Most of the information in this book has been culled from the pages of "The Commercial Motor" and "Motor Traction" of the years in question; some has also been obtained from studying photographs kindly supplied by Mr. D.E. Brewster from his extensive collection.

SIZE OF BUS FLEETS 1905–8

	1905		1906			1907		1908	
	July	Oct.	May	July	Oct.	May	Oct.	May	Oct.
Pioneer	9	11	14	21	—	63	—	—	—
Tilling	12	13	22	31	31	32	34	32	36
Birch	3	4	10	15	15	15	16	—	—
LGOC	4	12	63	84	129	169	197	253	285
Union Jack	19	32	68	90	121	160	205	235	242
Vanguard	16	36	108	147	159	310	366	371	387
Star	3	4	16	22	—	24	—	—	—
H. Turner	2	2	5	5	—	—	—	—	—
Kingsway	2	—	8	9	—	—	—	—	—
French	1	—	2	2	—	1	—	—	—
Associated	1	3	17	21	—	—	—	—	—
London County	1	—	—	—	—	—	—	—	—
Great Eastern	—	2	20	36	46	50	55	80	74
Arrow	—	—	38	43	—	—	—	—	—
Met. Steam	—	—	—	—	—	—	—	20	—
Central	—	—	—	—	—	5	6	13	16
Electrobus	—	—	—	—	—	—	6	12	19
Amalgamated	—	—	—	—	—	3	4	4	5
Burtwell	—	—	3	6	6	3	4	3	—
Newman	—	—	1	2	—	3	3	3	3
Balls Bros.	—	—	1	2	—	1	2	1	—
P. Hearn	—	—	5	6	—	9	—	—	—
Victoria	—	—	7	7	—	9	—	—	—
Standard	—	—	7	—	—	—	—	—	—
Sharland	—	—	3	4	—	—	—	—	—
T. Hearn	—	—	2	3	—	3	—	—	—
Rapide	—	—	12	—	—	—	—	—	—
Mellish & Boffin	—	—	2	2	—	—	—	—	—
Pilot	—	12	—	—	—	—	—	—	—
Atlas & Waterloo	—	3	—	—	—	—	—	—	—
Ensign	—	—	—	4	—	—	—	—	—

BREAKDOWN OF MAKES OF CHASSIS 1905–8

	1905 Oct.	1906 May	1906 July	1907 May	1907 Oct.	1908 May	1908 Oct.
SS–Büssing	3	98	146	265	334	347	366
Milnes-Daimler	64	172	221	296	322	310	312
De Dion	2	47	56	122	153	165	181
Wolseley	5	1	1	13	39	74	86
Arrol-Johnson	–	–	–	2	5	20	24
Darracq-Serpollet	–	–	–	–	1	20	20
Clarkson	1	11	23	3	7	15	13
Leyland	–	12	12	8	8	13	16
A. Whitworth	–	–	–	–	1	10	10
MOC (Mors)	–	–	–	9	8	7	7
Maudslay	–	–	1	6	6	6	6
Durkopp	–	28	29	31	1	11	18
Thornycroft	4	1	1	3	3	3	3
Dennis	–	2	1	4	6	6	6
Bellis & Morcom	–	–	–	–	–	1	1
Hallford	–	–	–	–	–	1	1
Lacoste & Battmann	–	1	8	24	2	1	–
Scott-Stirling	9	14	21	63	–	–	–
Scheibler	–	5	11	20	–	–	–
Brillié	1	10	15	15	–	–	–
Orion	4	9	9	9	–	–	–
Beaufort	–	–	–	2	–	–	–
Ducommun	–	10	4	–	–	–	–
Germain	13	1	2	–	–	–	–
Turgan	–	–	1	–	–	–	–
B.T.H.	–	–	–	–	1	1	–

NOTES ON MANUFACTURERS OF LONDON BUS CHASSIS

Straker Squire/Büssing: undoubtedly the most important chassis in the early years. The firm of Brazil & Holborow, engineers, set up at Avonside, Bristol, in 1893 and in 1897 moved to St. Philips Marsh to make steam vehicles. In 1899 Sidney Straker joined the firm and in 1901 the Straker Steam Vehicle Co. Ltd. was set up. In 1905 co-incident with the acquisition of the rights in the German Büssing petrol vehicle the firm was re-named Sidny Straker & Squire Ltd., The original 24 h.p. chassis proved so popular for buses, especially in London, that in 1906 a move was made to a larger factory at Fishponds; the 34 h.p. model came out, and in mid-1906 the 40 h.p. All were chain-driven and characterised by the radiator being mounted low between the frames in front of the bonnet. Later the firm developed its own chassis, and some were operated in London by Great Eastern.

Milnes-Daimler: an alliance between G.F. Milnes of Birkenhead and the German Daimler factory at Cannstatt. Final drive was by pinion and a toothed ring on the rear wheels, which became noisy when worn. Some were converted to Dennis worm drive.

De Dion: de Dion et Bouton of Puteaux, France. A feature was the rigid rear carrying axle, with differential on chassis and drive by half-shaft to each wheel. The wooden frame was said to give resiliance.

Thornycroft: J & I Thornycroft & Co. Ltd., steam vehicle makers of Chiswick, started with a petrol-engined design having a solid rear axle driven by one heavy chain and also carrying a band-brake. This was not very successful, and a new design came out in 1905 having twin chain drive; the chains drove 'carriers' made of leaf-spring attached to the rims of the wheels, thus avoiding strain on the felloes. In 1906 Thornycroft announced they would make no more buses for London.

Wolseley: the Wolseley Tool & Motor Co. of Adderley Park, started with a design having two-cylinder horizontal engine and side chain drive throughout. This did badly, and later in 1905 a design was introduced with 4-cylinder vertical Siddeley engine and shaft drive to final twin chains.

Leyland: the Lancashire Steam Motor Co. Ltd., makers of steam lorries and steam lawn mowers of Leyland, Lancs. The first petrol buses had Crossley engines; in 1906 Leyland introduced the familiar design with lowered radiator topped by a very large cast header-tank; live-axle drive.

Dennis: Dennis Bros. of Guildford specialised in the 'silent' worm-drive back axle and deserved better success than they had in London.

Scheibler: Automobiles T. Scheibler of Aix la Chapelle, a standard 35 H.P. Continental design, not taken up in any numbers.

Germain: S.A. des Ateliers Germain, Monceau-sur-Sambre, Belgium; a bad design with horizontal engine and driver seated above it; underpowered and off London streets at the end of 1906.

Ducommun: Ducommun et Cie, Mulhouse, France. The few examples in London seem to have been unreliable, and the Motor Car Emporium Ltd., who handled them. turned to selling Durkopps.

Brillié: Eugene Brillié of Paris, a typical French design with driver sitting over the engine; probably unreliable, as "Star" who operated most of them, gave up motor buses.

Beaufort: the Beaufort Motor Co. of Twickenham; a normal chain drive design which it seems did not appeal to the licensing authorities, supposedly on width, but there was also a long wheelbase.

Durkopp: Durkoppenwerke of Bielefeld, Germany; a solid design with chain drive.

Orion: this Swiss design had a horizontal engine; the first design was very light but later buses, as used by "Victoria" performed adequately.

BT-H : (British Thomson – Houston) one of many petrol-electric designs of the day, this one with Wolseley-Siddeley power, and rather heavy on petrol (about 7 m.p.g.). Not taken up.

Stoewer: Stoewer Motoren Werke of Stettin, Germany; not favoured.

Mors: a Paris firm handled in the U.K. by the Motor Omnibus Company and often called an MOC. Not numerous, probably due to agency difficulties.

Arrol-Johnston: a driver-beside-engine design which did not arrive in numbers until 1908 and seems to have lasted well; made in Paisley, Scotland.

Clarkson: this Chelmsford steam-bus manufacturer persisted with a very workable basic design. Early models were driver-over-engine, but later ones had the water-tube boiler housed in a normal bonnet, and although not taken up in large numbers, were working under "National" colours until 1919. Everyone spoke well of the Clarksons; the driver of Sharland No. 5 even wrote to the press in praise of them. A Mr. George Choat, of the Road Car Co. and later the LGOC, tentatively floated a company called The Steam Omnibus & Motor Co. Ltd. to operate them, as he "saw the shortcomings of the vehicles in use", but it seems not to have got off the ground.

Maudslay: the firm did not start until 1905 and missed the best of the market, but was producing good chain-drive buses by mid-1906.

Bellis & Morcom: well-known steam engineers who seem to have produced only one steam bus for London.

Hallford: old-established engineers, J. & E. Hall of Dartford manufactured under license the Swiss Saurer; they had early associations with Tillings, produced the Hallford-Stevens petrol- electric chassis.

Scott-Stirling: this Twickenham firm built all the buses for the "Pioneer" fleet; starting with small single-deckers, they came to making double-deckers with double-radiators up in front of the driver, and in later examples, iron wheels. Not taken up by any other fleet in London, but with some sixty "Pioneers" running, a leading U.K. make in numbers.

Turgan: Turgan-Foy of Lavallois, France; only one (40 H.P.) believed to have run in London.

Rolls-Metallurgique: Society Metallurgique d'Anvers, Belgium; only one bus.

Armstrong-Whitworth: a later comer; at least 10 buses ran but details are not available. Sir W.G. Armstrong-Whitworth of Elswick, Newcastle.

Lacoste-Battman: Lacoste et Battman of Levallois, France; a normal chain drive vehicle operated only in small numbers.

Darracq-Serpollet: Darracq of Suresnes and Serpollet of Paris; a steam design with water-tube boiler, sound in design but complicated to drive and maintain. Could make frightening roaring noises if badly handled.

Cremorne: the Cremorne Motor Manufacturing Co. of Chelsea provided only one chassis for a London bus, too light for general adoption.

Ryknield: the Ryknield Motor Co. Ltd., Burton-on-Trent; this design had the same toothed-ring final drive as the Daimler, but was powerful and well-built; only one example is known to have run in London.